A Taste of culture

FOODS OF MEXICO

Barbara Sheen

KIDHAVEN PRESS

An imprint of Thomson Gale, a part of The Thomson Corporation

THOMSON

GALE

Detroit • New York • San Francisco • San Diego • New Haven, Conn. • Waterville, Maine • London • Munich

THOMSON

━━━━━━━✦━━━━━━━ ™

GALE

For more information, contact
KidHaven Press
27500 Drake Rd.
Farmington Hills, MI 48331-3535
Or you can visit our Internet site at http://www.gale.com

LIBRARY OF CONGRESS CATALOGING-IN-PUBLICATION DATA

Sheen, Barbara.
  Foods of Mexico / by Barbara Sheen.
    p. cm. — (A taste of culture)
  Includes bibliographical references and index.
  ISBN 0-7377-3036-6 (hardcover : alk. paper)
  1. Cookery, Mexican. 2. Mexico—Social life and customs. I. Title. II. Series.
  TX716.M4S455 2005
  394.1'2'0972—dc22
 	
                                                                      2004028791

Printed in the United States of America

6/07

Contents

The Backbone of Mexican Cooking

When people think about Mexican food, three essential ingredients come to mind: corn, beans, and chile peppers. These three ingredients have been the backbone of Mexican cooking for centuries.

All-Important Corn

Corn has always been Mexico's main crop. Mexicans use corn in almost everything, from main dishes to snacks, soups, desserts, and beverages. It is hard to find a Mexican recipe that does not contain corn. "In no other part of America or of the world has corn been utilized in so many delicious forms,"[1] Mexican chef C. Gandia de Fernandez explains.

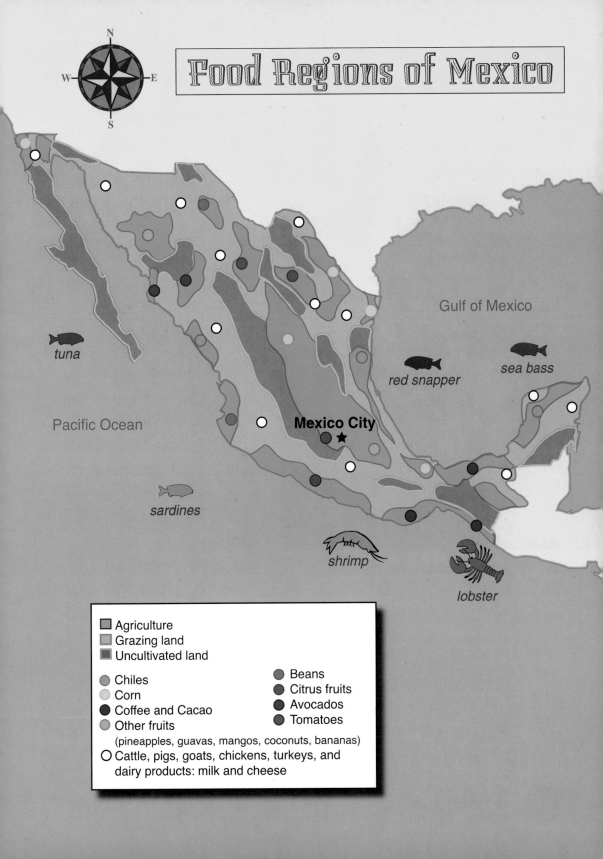

Dozens of varieties of corn, each a different size, color, and flavor, grow in Mexico. Tall corn, short corn, sweet corn, popping corn, white corn, yellow corn, and blue corn fill fields in northern and central Mexico.

Essential Tortillas

Sweet corn is roasted for corn on the cob. Popping corn becomes popcorn. White and yellow corn kernels are used in stews. But Mexicans grind much of the corn into **masa**, a type of cornmeal used to make **tortillas**, the soft, round flat bread eaten all across Mexico.

These farmers in the town of Veracruz are harvesting ears of corn, Mexico's most important crop.

Mexicans eat tortillas at every meal. They butter tortillas, roll them around various fillings, dip them in sauces, warm them in casseroles, drop them into soups, and munch on them for snacks. Each Mexican eats about 228 pounds (103kg) of tortillas a year.

Many Mexicans make their own tortillas. And, bakeries that specialize in making tortillas, called **tortillerias**, produce thousands of tortillas every day. Each village has at least one tortilleria, and bigger towns and cities often have dozens.

Tortillas are not baked in an oven. Instead, bakers shape masa dough into thin round disks and heat them on a griddle known as a **comal** until they are golden. "Hot off the griddle," a traveler in Mexico recalls, "they melted in the mouth, leaving a lingering taste of corn."[2]

An Ancient Plant

Corn, which originated in Mexico 80,000 years ago, has been an essential part of Mexican cooking for thousands of years. The Aztecs who ruled Mexico from the 12th to the 16th century, depended on corn. Sixteenth-century drawings of Aztec life depict native women making tortillas and selling them in the marketplace.

Beans

Beans have been a part of Mexican cooking as long as corn. No meal in Mexico is complete without them. Although Mexicans have a large variety of beans to choose from, their favorites are pink-speckled pinto beans and black beans.

Each Mexican eats about 33 pounds (15kg) of beans per year. Because Mexicans use such large quantities of beans, they are typically sold dried in burlap sacks that hold up to 100 pounds (45kg). Shoppers can also scoop out any amount of beans that they want from large barrels found in supermarkets, corner markets, and outdoor marketplaces.

Slowly Simmered or Refried

To prepare beans, Mexicans cook them slowly in a large earthenware pot called an **olla**. The olla is filled with wa-

Mexican Beans

Mexican-style beans are soft and creamy. Although they take time to cook, they are easy to prepare. Cooks can add sliced potato, garlic, tomato, and a pinch of oregano and epazote to the cooking pot depending on their taste. In this recipe, the beans are cooked in an electric slow cooker. They can also be cooked in the traditional way on the stove at low heat until they are soft.

Ingredients:

1 pound dry pinto beans
6 cups of water
half of an onion, chopped
1 can chopped green chiles
1 teaspoon salt

Instructions:

1. Wash the beans and pick out any small stones.
2. Soak the beans in a pot of water overnight.
3. Throw out the water and put the beans in an electric slow cooker. Cover the beans with six cups of water, or about three-fourths of the way full.
4. Add the other ingredients.
5. Cook over low heat until the beans are soft, four to six hours.

Serve hot in bowls with tortillas on the side.

Serves 8

A woman in Mexico City prepares corn tortillas, while a pot of beans simmers on the stove in the background.

ter; a pinch of salt; a few tablespoons of **lard**, a shortening made from pork fat; chopped onions; and an herb called epazote. The epazote gives the beans a nutty flavor.

Slow cooking makes the beans tender. Mexicans eat beans for breakfast, as a side dish at lunch, as an after-school snack, and for a light dinner. Beans are used in soups and stews, mixed with rice, and piled on tortillas. Or they may be mashed and fried in their own broth until they form a flavorful paste known as refried beans. It is hard to imagine a Mexican kitchen that does not have a pot of beans cooking. Marlena Spieler, a cookbook author

Big piles of different kinds of beans are on display at an outdoor market in the town of Tepoztlan.

and a frequent visitor to Mexico, explains: "At almost any moment in most any kitchen in Mexico, simmering quietly on a back burner is the earthenware casserole known as 'olla' filled with soupy bubbling beans."[3]

A Healthy Combination

Mexicans have been eating beans for centuries. Beans were so essential to the Aztecs' diet that each Aztec village was required to pay a tribute of 8,000 bushels (281,600 liters) of beans to the Aztec emperor annually.

Like modern Mexicans, the Aztecs always combined beans with corn. This combination is extremely nutritious. Beans and corn both contain **amino acids**, the building blocks of protein. When they are combined, the amino acids in each food fit together perfectly, providing the body with a plentiful supply of protein to build cells and muscles.

A Powerful Plant

Chile peppers add zest to this healthy combination. It is difficult to imagine Mexican food without them. Like

beans and corn, chiles have always been a part of the Mexican diet.

Chiles are so important, in fact, that over time Mexicans have attributed magical powers to the vegetables. Early Mexicans believed that eating chiles repelled witches, prevented the evil eye, and helped prevent disease. Although chiles do not have any magical powers, they are loaded with vitamins A, B, and C, which promote good health. In addition, chemicals in chiles destroy bacteria and fungi that cause food poisoning.

Bright, Colorful Chiles

Over 60 different varieties of this healthy vegetable grow in every part of Mexico. Some are hot and spicy. Some are sweet and mild. Chiles start out green, changing color as they ripen. Mexican fields are full of tiny red chile pequines, triangular blond gueros, and chubby orange habaneros, to name a few. Some, like the long, green poblano chile, are stuffed with meat or cheese and rolled in breading to make chile rellenos, a popular Mexican dish. Others, like the little green jalapeño, are pickled and served on the table with every meal. Most other chiles are used for spice or in sauces.

Roasted or Dried

Some Mexicans grow their own chiles, but most buy them in supermarkets,

A young woman strings bright red chiles together and hangs them in the sun to dry.

outdoor markets, and directly from farmers. Chiles are rarely eaten raw. They are roasted or dried before they are used. To dry chiles, Mexicans gather about two dozen ripe red chiles and tie one to the next, forming a long braid known as a **ristra**. It is hung in a warm, sunny place to dry. Ristras decorate sunny Mexican courtyards and doorways, where their bright color and pungent aroma welcome visitors. Once dried, cooks pluck chiles off the ristra, skin them, and grind them into a tangy powder.

Mexicans roast chiles on grills and in ovens. While they are roasting, a unique and delicious scent fills the air. Once roasted and peeled, chiles are ready for use in sauces, casseroles, and as toppings for many Mexican dishes. Mexican cooks always wear gloves when they peel chiles because oils concentrated in the chile and seeds of the chile can irritate or even burn a person's skin.

Salsa

Roasted or dried, one of the most common uses for chile is in making **salsa**, or sauce. Chiles and chile powder are added to ingredients like tomatoes, onions, garlic, lime juice, nuts, chocolate, mango, or tomatillos, which are a tomato-like fruit. They make flavorful sauces that are used as seasonings and toppings for everything from chicken and fish to tortillas and eggs. A Mexican table is considered bare without a bowl of salsa on it. "Without chile," Karen Blue, a longtime Mexican resident explains, "Mexicans don't believe they're eating. . . . If corn is the backbone of Mexican cooking, then chile is its soul."[4]

Tomato and Green Chile Salsa

A wide variety of ingredients can be used to make salsa. This recipe calls for cilantro, a popular Mexican herb. Most supermarkets sell it. Oregano can be used in its place. This salsa is a good dip for chips. It can be kept refrigerated for days.

Ingredients:

1 cup green chiles, chopped
half of an onion, chopped
4 tomatoes, chopped
juice of half of a lime
2 sprigs of cilantro
2 tablespoons water
salt and pepper to taste

Instructions:

1. Combine all ingredients in a bowl.
2. Chill for one hour.

Serves 4

A man and his daughter enjoy a tasty snack of roasted corn from a street vendor in Tijuana.

Indeed, Mexicans cannot live without their three favorite ingredients: chiles, corn, and beans. They make Mexican cooking the vividly colored, deliciously spicy, nutrient-packed food that everyone loves.

Chapter

2

A Delicious Blend

In the 16th century, the Spanish colonized Mexico. The Aztecs introduced the Spanish to many new foods. Corn, chiles, pinto beans, avocados, tomatoes, chocolate, and turkey are just a few. In exchange, the Spanish brought wheat, rice, limes, sugar, chicken, pork, beef, and dairy products to Mexico. Mexican cooks added the new ingredients to the old. In so doing, they created some of Mexico's favorite dishes.

Favorites vary among the different regions of Mexico. Seafood dishes are favored on the coasts. Tropical fruit dishes are beloved in the south, and beef dishes are popular in the north. But everyone adores enchiladas, guacamole, tortilla soup, and **ceviche**.

A Tortilla Dipped in Sauce

Enchiladas may be the most popular food in Mexico. Mexicans eat them morning, noon, and night. To make enchiladas, cooks grill or fry tortillas, dip them in chile sauce, roll them around a variety of fillings, and heat them until all the flavors blend together deliciously.

People in different parts of Mexico have different favorite fillings and sauces. Chile with cream sauce is popular in Mexico City. Ground pork mixed with zucchini is a preferred filling in the south, and grilled beef is a northern choice.

A cook in a Oaxaca restaurant spoons fillings into tortillas to prepare enchiladas, a very popular Mexican dish.

Creamy Green Enchiladas

Creamy enchiladas are popular in Mexico City. The cream helps balance the spicy taste.

Ingredients:

12 corn tortillas

1 can green enchilada sauce

1 can cream of mushroom soup

2 cups Monterey Jack or other white cheese, grated

1 tomato, chopped

1/4 cup onions, chopped

Instructions:

1. Put the green enchilada sauce in a pot with the cream of mushroom soup and stir. Do not add water.

2. Mix in the tomato and onions.

3. Cook over medium heat until it boils, stirring to avoid burning the sauce.

4. At the same time, heat oil in a frying pan.

5. Fry the tortillas one at a time in the oil until they are soft and hot. Do not fry until they are crisp or brown.

6. When each tortilla is done, remove it from the pan and drain it on a paper towel.

7. Dip each tortilla in the sauce.

8. Fill each tortilla with cheese and roll it up around the cheese. Place in a heated serving dish.

9. When all the tortillas are filled, pour the remaining sauce over them. Sprinkle with more cheese on top, and serve hot.

Serves 4

No matter where they live, Mexicans match the fillings and sauces so that their flavors complement each other. The taste and the color of the enchiladas change depending on what is used. One popular combination consists of shredded chicken and white cheese, topped with a sauce made from green chiles and cream. Another uses red chiles and tomatoes for the sauce and grilled chicken, onions, and sharp yellow cheese for the filling. A popular breakfast enchilada combines eggs and potatoes with a sauce of green chiles and onions. To prepare breakfast enchiladas, cooks scramble the eggs with the potatoes. Then they dip the tortilla in the sauce. Lastly they put the scrambled eggs on the tortilla and roll the tortilla around the filling.

A Social Ritual

To Mexicans, eating enchiladas is more than a delectable way to satisfy their hunger. It is a part of a social ritual that takes place in villages and cities throughout Mexico.

Mexicans traditionally stroll around their town **plazas** on warm evenings. When night falls, enchilada makers set up small stands in the plaza. When the mouthwatering scent becomes too enticing to resist, the

Enchiladas

walkers gather at long tables with plates of enchiladas, eating, talking, and laughing far into the night. Salvador, a Mexican boy, explains: "Enchiladas are a part of our culture. . . . They are also my favorite food."[5]

Guacamole: The Poor Man's Butter

Guacamole is another dish that Mexicans adore. Made from mashed avocados, guacamole is a rich, creamy treat.

Historians say avocados originated in Mexico, and the Aztecs were the first people to make guacamole. In fact, the word *guacamole* is an Aztec word.

Aztec peasants spread guacamole on tortillas just like modern people spread butter on bread. That may be why the Spanish called guacamole the poor man's butter.

Today, guacamole is eaten by everyone, rich or poor. It is used in dozens of ways—rolled inside a warm tortilla, drizzled on grilled meat, scooped on top of enchiladas, mixed with vinegar and fish, and as a side dish, salad, or dip for crisp-fried tortilla chips or pork rinds.

A Delicate Fruit

Guacamole is easy to make. Cooks mash the smooth, green avocado flesh until it is transformed into a creamy paste. Then they add their favorite seasonings, such as chopped green chiles, tomatoes, limes, and a sprig of cilantro, a Mexican herb.

A woman in Juarez mashes avocados in a large olla to make the creamy paste known as guacamole.

No matter what season-
ings are used, guacamole
must be eaten shortly after it
is made. This is because avocados are delicate fruits. When
exposed to air, chemicals in an avocado's flesh mix with oxygen in a pro-
cess called oxidation. When this occurs,
the avocado's flesh turns from bright green to brown, and
the guacamole loses its flavor. But when guacamole is
fresh, its vibrant color and rich taste are perfection. A
Mexican woman says, "There is no better way to savor an
avocado than in good guacamole."[6]

Wet and Dry Soups

Mexicans often eat guacamole with soup, another dish
they love. In fact, soup is so popular in Mexico that Mexicans have two different types of soup—wet soup and dry
soup. Wet soup is the hot liquid that Americans call soup.
Dry soup is broth-flavored rice, noodles, or tortillas.

Wet or dry, Mexicans adore soup. They frequently eat
a piping hot bowl of soup served with a stack of tortillas
for breakfast and supper. And soup is always served as
the first course at lunch, which is the largest meal of the
day. Mexicans do not consider lunch complete without it.

Nourishing Tortilla Soup

Because soup is so popular, Mexicans make a number
of delicious varieties. The one that most Mexicans trea-
sure is tortilla soup.

Guacamole

Guacamole is easy to make. Use ripe avocados that feel somewhat soft when you press their skin.

Ingredients:

3 ripe avocados
1 can chopped green chiles
1 small tomato, chopped
half of a small onion, chopped
juice of half of a lime
salt to taste

Instructions:

1. Cut the avocados in half horizontally. Remove the pit from the center.

2. Scoop the avocado out of the skin and put in a bowl.

3. Use a potato masher, fork, or the back of a spoon to mash the avocados.

4. Mix in the onion, tomato, chiles, and salt and mash some more.

5. Squirt with lime juice.

The guacamole can be smooth or coarse. It is ready when it can be scooped with a spoon. Serve the guacamole with chips or hot tortillas.

Serves 6

Tortilla soup is a chicken broth that is flavored with tomatoes, garlic, chiles, onions, limes, and epazote. What makes tortilla soup special is the pieces of fried tortillas that are added to the hot liquid before it is served. To make the taste even more interesting, a sprinkle of grated cheese and an avocado slice are often placed on the bottom of the bowl before the soup is ladled in.

Tortilla soup is very nourishing. Chicken broth contains amino acids that help repair the body, and the tomatoes, chiles, and limes provide lots of vitamin C. In Mexico, a hot bowl of tortilla soup is a common remedy for colds and flu. It is, according to Lorraine Russo, who lives in Mexico, "Mexico's comfort food."[7]

What Makes a Chile Hot?

Chiles contain a substance called capsaicin, which makes them hot. A chile's spiciness is determined by how much capsaicin it contains.

Food scientists measure a chile's heat in units called Scoville units. These units represent the amount of capsaicin a particular type of chile contains. The scale ranges from 0 to 550,000 units. The more units, the hotter the chile. For instance, the hottest chile is the habanero. It rates 100,000 to 350,000 Scoville units. The milder serrano chile, which is used in many Mexican recipes, contains between 7 and 25,000 units.

A Spanish Treat

Tortilla soup is one dish that the Aztecs missed out on. The Spanish introduced chicken broth to Mexico. To suit their love of spice, Mexicans added chiles and tomatoes. And because tortillas get stale quickly, adding them to the mix was a thrifty way for Mexican cooks to make use of tortillas that were no longer fresh. Their lack of freshness is undetectable when they are added to the soup. Instead, they add a unique corn taste that Mexicans love.

Ceviche

Ceviche, a fish dish, is another Mexican favorite. It reminds Mexicans of the beach.

Mexico has over 3,700 miles (5,954m) of coastline. Its waters teem with every type of seafood imaginable. Every coastal village has at least one waterfront restaurant that is famous for its mariscos, or seafood. Vacationing Mexicans and coastal dwellers flock to these eateries. The food they crave is ceviche.

A fisher on the Sea of Cortez returns from a long day of fishing. Mexico is famous for its seafood.

Ceviche is made of fresh raw fish, such as red snapper or sea bass, that is marinated in lime juice and spiced with chiles, tomatoes, and onions. The fish marinates for about an hour. During this time, acids in the lime juice

A woman at a roadside stand in Cabo San Lucas dishes up a delicious bowl of hot tortilla soup.

Gorditas, Tostadas, and Chalupas

Gorditas, tostadas, and chalupas, are favorite Mexican dishes that use masa or tortillas as their main ingredient. Gorditas, which means "little fat ones," and chalupas, which means "little canoes," are masa cakes that are fried and then molded to form round or pointed "bowls." They are then filled with ingredients such as beans, cheese, chiles, pork, sausage, beef, or chicken.

Tostadas are fried tortillas topped with beans, salsa, cheese, chicken, and avocado. In central Mexico, pickled pig's feet mixed with onions, garlic, jalapeños, and vinegar are a popular tostada topping.

When fried tortillas are broken into small triangles, they are known as tostaditas, or little tostadas. These are known in the United States as tortilla chips. Mexicans dip tostaditas into salsa. They also top them with refried beans.

cook the fish without heat, changing the look and texture of it from pink to white, just as heat does.

Mexicans are careful to use only the freshest fish to make ceviche. Less-than-fresh fish tastes mushy and can cause food poisoning. But when the fish is fresh, ceviche is delicious.

It Started with a Lime

Ceviche is not native to Mexico. But once limes were introduced, Mexican cooks paired them with seafood and chiles, and ceviche was born.

For Mexicans, a visit to the coast is incomplete without ceviche. Ceviche, according to Mexican cookbook author Rick Bayless, "makes folks feel the thick, salty-smelling coastal air with just one bite."[8]

Whether it is ceviche at a coastal café, enchiladas in the village plaza, guacamole in a fine restaurant, or tortilla soup in grandma's kitchen, Mexicans cannot resist these delicious dishes. Mexican cooks cleverly combined the native foods of their ancestors with the foods of the Spanish to create these savory dishes that every Mexican loves.

Snacks and Sweets

Mexicans love snacks and sweets. Wherever a person goes in Mexico, there are restaurants and street vendors tempting passersby with delicious treats. On beaches and in cities, parks, plazas, markets, schoolyards, and grandmothers' kitchens, the air is full of enticing aromas that Mexicans find hard to resist.

Tacos: Everyone's Favorite Snack

Tacos, which literally mean "light snacks," are far and away Mexico's favorite snack. Every neighborhood in Mexico has at least one **taqueria**. Here, hot grilled tortillas are wrapped around more than 100 different fillings, spiced with salsa, and garnished with onions, chiles, and limes. Unlike American-style tacos, Mexican

This woman is making tacos to sell at a taqueria in Tepoztlan. Tacos are a favorite snack in Mexico.

tacos use soft, warm tortillas rather than hard, fried shells.

Day or night, taquerias are crowded with people from every walk of life enjoying their favorite snack. Karen Hursh Graber, the food writer for the *News*, a Mexico City newspaper, and a longtime Mexican resident, explains: "Everyone eats them. From fashionably dressed couples munching on grilled beef tacos at sidewalk tables to day laborers."[9]

Taco

Anything that can be crammed inside a corn tortilla can fill a taco. Like enchiladas, Mexicans have regional favorites, but some fillings are popular everywhere. These include grilled beef, beef tongue, pork marinated in chile sauce, scrambled eggs with potatoes, shredded chicken, spicy sausage, and fresh fish.

To make tacos, corn tortillas and fillings are cooked on a charcoal grill or on a **plancha**, a griddle made out of a piece of rolled steel. Meat fillings are always thinly cut. Fish fillings are made from shrimp or bite-size pieces of white fish. Onions and chiles brown and sizzle on the plancha, too. The filling, onions, chiles, and salsa are then spooned onto the hot tortilla, which is folded and topped with a squeeze of lime juice.

A Perfect Snack for Busy People

Tacos are a perfect snack for busy people. There is no need for utensils. This may be why Aztec peasants loved tacos, which they ate filled with fish, beans, squash, grasshoppers, and other small insects. Although the fillings have changed, each day millions of Mexicans eat tacos. Tacos are, Rick Bayless explains, "woven into the fabric of Mexican life."[10]

A Special Gift

When Mexicans want a sweet treat, they drink hot chocolate, a treat that has been a Mexican favorite since before the Spanish arrived. **Cacao** trees, which produce the cacao bean from which chocolate is made, are native to Mexico. In fact, chocolate was unknown in the rest of the world until the Spanish explorers acquired it from the Aztecs.

Chocolate has always been important to Mexicans. The Mayas, who ruled in Mexico before the Aztecs, roasted and ground cacao beans, producing a thick paste that they mixed with hot water, ground almonds, and honey. This early form of hot chocolate, although not as sweet as the chocolate used today, was precious to the Maya. They believed that their god, Quetzalcoatl, gave the cacao tree to the Maya as a special gift.

Sweet and Frothy

Today, hot chocolate is served in every Mexican home. And street vendors, cafés, and restaurants tempt passersby with a sweet, steaming treat. Most Mexicans buy packages of hard chocolate tablets that they mix with milk or water to make hot chocolate. Some Mexicans still grind their own chocolate much like some Americans grind coffee. Mexican grocery stores have special grinders that grind cacao beans, almonds, sugar, and cinnamon into an irresistibly sweet syrup. Mexicans put the syrup into disk-shaped molds in the sun to harden. Once solid, cooks chop the chocolate disk, mix

Mexican Hot Chocolate

Mexican hot chocolate is not as sweet as hot cocoa, but it is rich and delicious. This recipe calls for Mexican chocolate, but sweet cooking or baker's chocolate can be used instead.

Ingredients:

6 ounces Mexican chocolate or 6 ounces cooking chocolate broken into small pieces
4 cups milk
1 teaspoon cinnamon

Instructions:

1. Put all the ingredients in a pot and cook it over low heat, stirring constantly until the chocolate is melted. Allow the mixture to get hot, but do not boil.
2. Remove from the stove and mix with an electric mixer until it becomes foamy.
3. Pour in cups and drink hot.

Serves 4

A boy in Tabasco spreads cacao beans to dry in the sun. Cacao beans have been a part of Mexican culture since Mayan times.

it with hot milk or water, and whip it with a **molinillo**, a special wooden beater that cooks twirl between their palms. This causes a foamy froth to form. Mexicans say that the thicker the foam, the better the hot chocolate. According to Nancy Zaslavsky, Mexican cookbook author, "Mexicans believe the spirit of the drink is in the foam."[11]

Flan

Mexicans drink hot chocolate at least twice a day, year-round. It is popular for breakfast as well as for a mid-morning, late afternoon, or midnight snack, much in the same way coffee is in the United States. In fact, hot chocolate shops are crowded night and day with thirsty Mexicans.

Flan: Mexico's Favorite Dessert

Mexicans say that nothing goes better with a cup of hot chocolate or a plate of tacos than **flan**, a sugary yellow custard topped with a creamy caramel crust. Served everywhere from street carts to home kitchens, flan is a comforting and much-loved dessert.

Prepared in individual custard cups, flan is made from sugar, milk, eggs, and vanilla. It originated in Spain, but Mexicans made it their own by adding vanilla, a spice that comes from Mexico. The addition of vanilla gives Mexican flan a delicious fragrance and flavor.

Flan is so popular in Mexico that stores sell instant flan mixes for busy cooks. But many Mexicans still prepare flan the old-fashioned way.

Syrup and Custard

To make flan, cooks heat sugar in a skillet until it turns gold and **carmelizes**—that is, it turns into a pale syrup. The syrup is poured into custard cups and is spread over the sides of the cups. Next, a mixture of eggs, milk, sugar, and vanilla is poured in. The flan is then baked

Churros: A Mexican Snack

Churros are fluted strips of dough that are fried and covered with sugar and cinnamon. Bakeries and street vendors throughout Mexico entice customers with this sweet pastry.

To make a churro, a baker spoons dough into a churrera—a tool similar to a pastry bag or cake-decorating tube with a star-shape or fluted tip. The baker squeezes about 4 inches (10cm) of dough out of the churrera at a time, dropping it into a frying pan full of hot oil. When the churro turns golden brown, it is removed from the pan, rolled in cinnamon and sugar, and eaten hot.

Even though churros are typically eaten right out of the frying pan, their unique pleated shape keeps them from absorbing too much oil and tasting greasy. Instead, they are crisp on the outside and soft on the inside, similar in taste and texture to a doughnut. Their crisp skin makes them perfect for dunking in hot chocolate, which is what Mexicans love to do.

A bakery in Oaxaca offers many of the tasty treats that Mexicans enjoy for dessert.

and refrigerated. Cooling the flan sets it, changing it from a wiggly mass similar to Jell-O to satiny custard. Before flan is served, the custard cups are turned upside down. As the flan is released, the caramel syrup runs over it. The result—a satiny custard that tastes of sugar and cream—is a perfect way to cool the tongue after a spicy meal. "Each and every flan is sheer heaven,"[12] Elaine Sosa, a Mexican woman, explains.

Milk-Drenched Cake

When Mexicans want a special dessert, their top choice is **tres leche cake**, or three-milk cake. No dinner party or banquet is complete without this delectable treat.

Tres leche cake is a delicious, buttery sponge cake. What makes it unique and gives it a sweet, moist taste is that the cake is soaked in three milk products—whole milk or cream, sweetened condensed milk, and evaporated milk.

To make tres leche cake, cooks bake or buy a sponge cake. Then they poke small holes all over the cake with a fork and pour the three different milks over it. The cake absorbs the different milky flavors through the small holes without getting mushy.

Delicious Toppings

Bakers ice the cake with a variety of toppings. Whipped cream and fresh fruit are common. Coconut is also a favorite, and some Mexicans, especially those in the tropical south, use coconut milk in place of whole milk. This gives the cake an exotic, nutty flavor.

Perhaps the most popular topping is cajeta, a caramel sauce made from sugar and goat milk. But no matter what topping is chosen, tres leche

Tres Leche Cake

Tres leche cake can either be prepared from scratch or a yellow cake mix can be used. To make the preparation even simpler, a store-bought sponge or pound cake can also be used. Fresh peaches, strawberries, or other fruit can be placed on the top of the cake over the whipped cream, if desired.

Ingredients:

1 yellow cake mix
1 cup milk
6 ounces sweetened condensed milk
6 ounces evaporated milk
whipped cream

Instructions:

1. Bake the cake following the package instructions.

2. Pierce the cake with a fork on the top and sides in about fifteen places.

3. Let the cake cool. Put on a platter.

4. Combine the three different milks. Pour them over the top of the cake. Move the cake to a dry plate.

5. Refrigerate the cake for at least 2 hours. Keep cake refrigerated until ready to serve.

6. Before serving, spread the whipped cream over the top of the cake.

7. To avoid spoiling the milk in the cake, keep the cake refrigerated at all times.

cake is always a treat. A woman recalls that the first time her family tasted the rich dessert, "We wanted to lick the plates but thought it rude."[13]

With tres leche cake, custardy flan, steamy hot chocolate, and mouth-watering tacos tempting them, it is no

Spicy and Sweet

Mexicans love sweets. But there is nothing they love more than the taste of chile peppers. To satisfy their two passions, Mexicans have created a variety of unique snacks that combine their two favorite flavors—sweet and spicy.

One of their favorite combinations is a fresh mango topped with chile powder. In warm weather, street vendors peel and cut the sweet, juicy tropical fruit so that it looks like a bright yellow flower. They then put it on a stick and sprinkle it with red-hot chile powder. The sweet and hot flavors mix to create a singularly delicious taste. Mexicans walk through the street nibbling on this tropical treat in the same way that people in the United States might eat a popsicle.

wonder Mexicans love snacks and desserts. Every restaurant, street vendor, and kitchen in Mexico offers hungry Mexicans another tempting treat that is hard to resist.

Chapter 4

Food for Special Occasions

Mexicans celebrate important occasions and holidays with special foods. These special days would not be the same without the unique foods that always accompany them.

Christmas Tamales

Eating **tamales** at Christmas is a Mexican tradition. Tamales are steamy corn pockets filled with spicy or sweet ingredients and wrapped, like little packages, in corn husks or banana leaves. Making tamales requires that cooks soak and clean the corn husks or banana leaves, make and knead the dough, cook and shred the meat and other fillings, prepare the sauce, and then assemble and steam the tamales. It is time-consuming

This Mexican family is ready to enjoy the delicious tamales that they all worked hard to prepare.

and difficult work, which may be why tamales are reserved for special occasions.

Before Christmas, many Mexican families get together and have a **tamalada**, a tamale-making party. Forming an assembly line, young and old family members have fun working together to prepare tamales. Diana Kennedy, an expert on Mexican cooking who has lived in Mexico most of her life, explains: "Tamales are made for an occasion, and an occasion is made of making them."[14]

Different Varieties

Tamales are filled with all the ingredients Mexicans love. Beef with green chiles, refried beans with cheese, shredded chicken with red chile sauce, pork with pineapple, and pumpkin with raisins are just a few of the mouth-watering choices.

There are also regional differences. Fish, shrimp, and iguana are popular fillings along the coast. Beef with corn and chiles is a northern specialty, and fruit tamales are a tropical favorite.

Like Christmas gifts, tamales come in every shape and size. They can be thin and rectangular, short and boxy, or gigantic. The Huasteca of central Mexico are famous for their 3-foot (0.9m) long, 150-pound (68kg) tamale, which is made for a festival and takes all the leaves of a banana tree to wrap.

Making Tamales

Despite their shape, size, or filling, to make tamales, cooks must first make dough using masa. They fold the dough over the filling to form a little bundle that is carefully wrapped in a corn husk or banana leaf and is tied closed. The tamales are then stacked in a large pot and are steamed until they are hot and delicious.

Tamales are made in four basic steps. First dough is spread onto corn husks (1). Next, a flling is spread on the dough (2). Then the corn husks are folded, tied, and steamed (3). Finally the flavorful bundles are served steaming hot (4).

They are served wrapped in their husks, like perfect little Christmas packages. When diners unwrap the tamales, they are greeted by a burst of steam and a luscious aroma, which, to Mexicans, is Christmas. Evadina, a woman whose family comes from Mexico, explains: "When I think of Christmas, I think of tamales."[15]

Atole

Mexicans traditionally sip **atole** as they eat their Christmas tamales. Atole is a corn-based beverage made by blending together water, milk, sugar, and masa. The masa gives atole a porridgelike consistency.

Atole can be drunk warm or cold, although hot atole is traditionally served at Christmas. Fresh fruit, chocolate, chiles, or nuts are often

Strawberry Atole

Atole is simple to make. The recipe calls for Masa Harina, a common brand of masa. Cornstarch can be substituted for masa. Blueberries or pineapple can be substituted for strawberries.

Ingredients:

1 cup Masa Harina
3 cups water
3 cups milk
1 cup strawberries, cleaned and chopped
$1/3$ cup sugar

Instructions:

1. Put the strawberries in the blender and puree.
2. Put the masa, milk, water, and sugar in a mixing bowl and stir until the lumps are gone.
3. Put the masa mix in a pot and cook over low heat, stirring constantly for three or four minutes or until the mix thickens.
4. Stir in the strawberry puree, and let the mix cook for another minute, stirring constantly.

The atole is done when it is thick, but not so thick that it cannot be poured into a cup.

Serves 6

blended with the other ingredients in order to give the atole a unique flavor and color.

Chocolate atole is called champurrado. It is thick and brown. Other popular atoles are purple blackberry atole, sweet and spicy red chile atole, pink strawberry atole, and yellow pineapple atole.

A Traditional Beverage

Mexicans have been drinking atole for centuries. Both the Maya and Aztec enjoyed the thick, comforting drink, which they prepared with water, masa, honey, chiles, and, often, beans. Today, atole welcomes guests to Christmas dinners and parties throughout Mexico. Evadina says, "I can't imagine Christmas without tamales and atole."[16]

Feasting with the Dead

Like Christmas, the Day of the Dead is another important Mexican holiday that is marked with special food. Celebrated on November 2, it is a festive day when Mexicans honor loved ones who have died. To celebrate the lives of those who have passed on, families have picnics in cemeteries and build little altars in memory of deceased family members in their homes. They place a skull-shaped candy and bread, known as bread of the dead, on the altar.

The Bread of Kings

Mexicans celebrate Three Kings' Day, which occurs twelve days after Christmas. On this day, Mexicans have dinner parties at which a sweet bread called rosca de reyes, or "bread of kings," is served. A tiny doll is baked somewhere inside the bread. According to Mexican tradition, whoever finds the doll must give a party for all the people present.

A family in Valladolid poses for a photo before sitting down to enjoy their Christmas feast of tamales.

Formed to look like a life-size skull with raisins or chiles for eyes, the bread is flavored with cinnamon and anise seed, a licorice-flavored herb. The candy skulls are made of sugar or chocolate. They can be life-size or bite-size. The dead person's name is written across both the candy and the bread skulls in icing. The names of the surviving loved ones are also written on the skulls.

A Reminder of Life

It is unknown where the tradition of edible skulls comes from. Historians know that the Aztecs offered

Day of the Dead Sugar Skulls

Making these sugar skulls is a combination cooking and art project. The cook can decorate them with any color food coloring or icing he or she likes. The skulls may be made large or small.

Ingredients:

2 cups powdered sugar
1 tablespoon light corn syrup
$1/4$ cup cornstarch
$1/2$ teaspoon vanilla extract
1 egg white
food coloring
colored sugar

Instructions:

1. Put the egg white, vanilla, and corn syrup in a bowl and mix together.
2. Add the sugar and mix until it forms a paste.
3. Form the mixture into a ball.
4. Sprinkle cornstarch on a cutting board.
5. Put the sugar mixture on the cutting board and knead it and roll it in the cornstarch.
6. Form the mixture into a ball, wrap it in plastic wrap, and refrigerate it for one hour.
7. When chilled, form the sugar mixture into round skull shapes. Use fingers to sculpt depressions for the eyes and nose.
8. Use a small paint brush and food coloring to paint the skulls.
9. Use cake icing and colored sugar to add additional decorations.
10. Let the skulls dry before eating.

human skulls to their gods. The Spanish, too, associated skulls with death. But no one can say where the idea of eating skull-shaped food arose.

No matter the origin, when families return from the cemetery, they have a big feast in which the bread and candy skulls are served. Ana, a Mexican teenager, explains: "We eat sugar candy shaped like skulls . . . that often have your name written on it. I guess this sounds weird or macabre to a foreigner, but to us Mexicans it's a celebration that we're still alive."[17]

For the Day of the Dead, Mexicans write the names of loved ones who have died on colorful, edible candy skulls.

Mole: An Interesting Blend

The main course at the Day of the Dead feast is usually turkey **mole**. This uniquely Mexican dish is the national dish of Mexico. But because mole can contain as many as 50 different ingredients and is quite difficult to make, it is reserved for important occasions such as the Day of the Dead.

Mole is a smooth, dark sauce made from chiles, onions, tomatoes, tomatillos, ground nuts and seeds, dried fruit, spices, and a little bit of chocolate. The flavors

A family in Michoacan offers gifts of food and flowers to honor the dead during the Day of the Dead celebration.

combine to form a rich and tangy sauce that turkey or chicken is cooked in. Mexican philosopher Alfredo Ramos Espinosa comments, "The very thought of it makes your mouth water."[18]

A Big Task

To make mole, cooks must juggle dozens of ingredients. Seeds and nuts must be toasted, chopped, and ground. Chocolate must be finely chopped. Chiles must be peeled, seeded, and fried. Tomatillos must be roasted. The turkey must be boiled and deboned. Then, everything is combined in a large stew pot and is allowed to cook for hours.

The taste and color changes depending on the type of chile and the ingredients used. Mole can be brown, red, or orange. But no matter what the color is, the result is a perfect balance of sweet and spicy. Rick Bayless recalls, "When I first let a spoonful of classic Mexican red mole bathe my tongue, it was an experience comparable to taking in the vista from the rim of the Grand Canyon—singular, breathtaking."[19]

A Happy Mistake

The exact origin of mole is unknown. The basic ingredients have been used for centuries by native Mexicans. But no one can say who was the first person to put them all together. One popular story says that Fray Pascual, a 15th-century Spanish priest living in Mexico,

Pozole

Pozole is another celebration food for Mexicans. Often eaten on New Year's Day, pozole is a hearty pork and hominy stew. Made from dried corn kernels, hominy is a traditional Mexican food.

To make pozole, the dried corn kernels are cooked until they soften. This takes about five hours. Then the pork is added. The pork used in traditional pozole comes from the pig's feet and head, but many Mexicans use pork shoulders and ribs instead. Salt, onions, and chiles are added to the pot. The stew cooks slowly, and it often takes all day before it is ready.

When the pozole is done, it is steamy hot. Chopped radishes, shredded cabbage, oregano, and lime slices are placed on the table for diners to add to their stew according to their taste. Hot tortillas and chips also accompany the stew.

was preparing a turkey dinner honoring the viceroy, the new Spanish governor of Mexico. A gust of wind caused a tray of spices and chocolate tablets to fall into the cooking pot, and turkey mole was born.

Today, the very thought of mole makes Mexicans want to celebrate. And celebrate they do, with mole, sugar skulls, and special bread on the Day of the Dead and tamales and atole on Christmas. These special foods make Mexican holidays fun and memorable.

Metric Conversions

Mass (weight)

1 ounce (oz.)	= 28.0 grams (g)
8 ounces	= 227.0 grams
1 pound (lb.) or 16 ounces	= 0.45 kilograms (kg)
2.2 pounds	= 1.0 kilogram

Liquid Volume

1 teaspoon (tsp.)	= 5.0 milliliters (ml)
1 tablespoon (tbsp.)	= 15.0 milliliters
1 fluid ounce (oz.)	= 30.0 milliliters
1 cup (c.)	= 240 milliliters
1 pint (pt.)	= 480 milliliters
1 quart (qt.)	= 0.95 liters (l)
1 gallon (gal.)	= 3.80 liters

Pan Sizes

8-inch cake pan	= 20 x 4-centimeter cake pan
9-inch cake pan	= 23 x 3.5-centimeter cake pan
11 x 7-inch baking pan	= 28 x 18-centimeter baking pan
13 x 9-inch baking pan	= 32.5 x 23-centimeter baking pan
9 x 5-inch loaf pan	= 23 x 13-centimeter loaf pan
2-quart casserole	= 2-liter casserole

Temperature

212° F	= 100° C (boiling point of water)
225° F	= 110° C
250° F	= 120° C
275° F	= 135° C
300° F	= 150° C
325° F	= 160° C
350° F	= 180° C
375° F	= 190° C
400° F	= 200° C

Length

1/4 inch (in.)	= 0.6 centimeters (cm)
1/2 inch	= 1.25 centimeters
1 inch	= 2.5 centimeters

Notes

Chapter 1: The Backbone of Mexican Cooking

1. Angeles de la Rosa and C. Gandia de Fernandez, *Flavors of Mexico*. San Francisco: 101 Productions, 1979, p. 43.
2. Quoted in Jeffrey M. Pilcher, *Que Vivan Los Tamales!* Albuquerque: University of New Mexico Press, 1998, p. 11.
3. Marlena Spieler, *Mexican Snacks*. Edison, NJ: Chartwell, 1996, p. 76.
4. Karen Blue and Lorraine Russo, "Living at Lake Chapala, Chile: A Mexican Staple," Mexico Insights, August 2002. www.mexico-insights.com/archives/kitchen.asp.

Chapter 2: A Delicious Blend

5. Quoted in Kid to Kid, "Enchiladas." http://danet.wicip.org/heron/gb2000/kid2kid.html.
6. Camille Collins, "Mexico Hot . . . or Not! Guacamole," Mexico Connect. www.mexconnect.com/mex_/recipes/list/guacen.html.
7. Lorraine Russo, "Living at Lake Chapala: Lorraine's Famous Tortilla Soup," Mexico Insights, January 2003. www.mexico-insights.com/archives/kitchen.asp.
8. Rick Bayless, *Mexico One Plate at a Time*. New York: Scribner, 2000, p. 11.

Chapter 3: Snacks and Sweets

9. Karen Hursh Graber, "Mexican Hot . . . or Not," Mexico Connect. www.mexconnect.com/mex_/recipes/puebla/kgtacos1.html.
10. Bayless, *Mexico One Plate at a Time*, p. 89.
11. Quoted in Susan Taylor, "Hot Chocolate Goes Upscale," *Detroit News*, October 26, 2000. www.detnews.com/2000/food/1026/lead/lead.htm.
12. Elaine Sosa, "Mexico City," Sally's Place. www.bpe.com/food_dining_directory/north_america/mexico_city.htm.
13. Quoted in FITDV Recipes, "Tres Leche Cake with Seasonal Fruit." www.fitdv.recipezaar.com/recipe/get.recipe.zsp?id=59323.

Chapter 4: Food for Special Occasions

14. Diana Kennedy, *The Essential Cuisines of Mexico*. New York: Clarkson Potter, 2000, p. 96.
15. Evadina, interview with the author, November 26, 2004, Las Cruces, New Mexico.
16. Evadina, interview.
17. Quoted in Think Quest, "Latin America." http://library.thinkquest.org/C002671F/latinam.html?tqskip1=1.
18. Quoted in Kennedy, *The Essential Cuisines of Mexico*, p. 325.
19. Bayless, *Mexico One Plate at a Time*, p. 204.

Glossary

amino acids: The building blocks of protein.

atole: A thick Mexican drink made with masa.

cacao: The bean from which chocolate is made.

carmelizes: When heated sugar becomes syrupy.

ceviche: A Mexican fish dish.

comal: A griddle upon which tortillas are cooked.

flan: Mexican custard.

lard: Pork fat used in cooking.

masa: Cornmeal.

mole: A sauce made with chiles, spices, and chocolate that is poured over poultry.

molinillo: A wooden beater that Mexicans twirl between their palms when making hot chocolate.

olla: An earthenware pot in which beans are cooked.

plancha: A sheet of metal upon which tacos are cooked.

plazas: The centers of towns or villages.

ristra: A long braid of chile peppers.

salsa: Mexican sauce, which usually contains chiles in its ingredients.

tamalada: A party at which tamales are made.

tamales: Corn pockets filled with spicy or sweet ingredients and wrapped in corn husks or banana leaves.

taqueria: A place where tacos are made.

tortillas: Flat Mexican bread made from masa.

tortillerias: Bakeries that specialize in making tortillas.

tres leche cake: A cake soaked in three types of milk.

For Further Exploration

Books

Deanna F. Cook, *The Kids' Multicultural Cookbook: Food and Fun Around the World.* Charlotte, VT: Williamson, 1995. This book contains recipes and fun facts from around the world, including Mexico.

Cheryl L. Enderlein, *Christmas in Mexico.* Mankato, MN: Capstone, 1998. Mexican Christmas customs, including holiday food, are discussed in this work.

Janice Hamilton, *Mexico in Pictures.* Minneapolis: Lerner, 2002. The author tells about the land, history, government, and culture of Mexico through pictures.

Sylvia A. Johnson, *Tomatoes, Potatoes, Corn, and Beans.* New York: Atheneum Books for Young Readers, 1997. This book talks about the origins of foods and how foods from Mexico and the Americas changed eating around the world.

Susan Milord, *Mexico: 40 Activities to Explore Mexico's Past and Present.* Charlotte, VT: Williamson, 1999. Mexican arts and crafts and cooking activities are explored in this book.

Marlena Spieler, *Mexican Snacks.* Edison, NJ: Chartwell, 1996. This is an adult cookbook that is simple enough for kids. It has lots of colorful illustrations and gives recipes for different types of tacos and other Mexican snacks.

Karen Ward, *The Young Chef's Mexican Cookbook*. New York: Crabtree, 2001. A simple Mexican cookbook for children.

Web Sites

Kids Konnect (www.kidskonnect.com/Mexico/Mexico Home.html). This site includes pictures, facts, and links all about Mexico just for kids.

Mexico Connect (www.mexicoconnect.com). This Web site offers pictures of different places in Mexico, geographic information, Mexican history, and information about holidays, festivals, culture, and Mexican food.

Mexico for Kids (www.elbalero.gob.mex/index_kids. html). A great site presented by the Mexican government, it offers information, pictures, games, and e-cards about Mexican history, government, geography, and daily life.

Think Quest (http://thinkquest.org/library/cat_show. html?cat_id=85). Among its many categories, this Web site for children has a section on cultures, countries, cuisines, and food history.

World Recipes (www.world-recipes.info). This site has recipes from all over the world. Click on Mexico to get Mexican recipes.

Index

Picture Credits

About the Author

Barbara Sheen has been an author and educator for more than 30 years. Her writing has been published in the United States and in Europe. She writes in both English and Spanish. She lives in New Mexico with her family. In her spare time, she likes to swim, walk, bike, garden, and cook. She especially likes cooking and eating Mexican food!